Twinkle Twinkle

The Number of Players: 2

The Object of the Game: To cover the last star on the board.

The Playing Pieces: Each player needs 10 identical playing pieces that are different from his or her opponent's. For example, you can use red and black checker pieces, doughnut-shaped and square cereal pieces, or dark and light buttons.

The Play: Players take turns covering 1 or 2 stars with their pieces. If 2 stars are covered, they must be next to each other.

The Winner: The player who covers the last star on the board wins.

There is a way to always be the winner. Think about whether it's better to go first or second. Think about what happens toward the end of each game.

Math Concepts: Logical reasoning. Addition and subtraction to 15.

I LOVE MATH

THE SEARCH FOR THE MYSTERY PLANET

SPACE MATH

TIME LIFE for Children ®

ALEXANDRIA, VIRGINIA

ALL ABOUT
I LOVE MATH

Discover why my checkers are floating away. See page 54.

The *I Love Math* series shows children that math is all around them in everything they do. It can be found at the grocery store, at a soccer game, in the kitchen, at the zoo, even in their own bodies. As you collect this series, each book will fill in another piece of your child's world, showing how math is a natural part of everyday activities.

What Is Math?

Math is much more than manipulating numbers; the goal of math education today is to help children become problem solvers. This means teaching kids to observe the world around them by looking for patterns and relationships, estimating, measuring, comparing, and using reasoning skills. From an early age, children do this naturally. They divide up cookies to share with friends, recognize shapes in pizza, measure how tall they have grown, or match colors and patterns as they dress themselves. Young children love math. But when math only takes the form of abstract formulas on worksheets, children begin to dislike it. The *I Love Math* series is designed to keep math natural and appealing.

How do pickles solve problems in space? Turn to page 34 to find out.

How Do Children Learn Math?

Research has shown that children learn best by doing. Therefore, *I Love Math* is a hands-on, interactive learning experience. The math concepts are woven into stories in which entertaining characters invite your child to help them solve math challenges. Activities reinforce the concepts, and parent notes offer ways you and your child can have more fun with this program.

We have worked closely with math educators to include in these books a full range of math skills. As the series progresses, repetition of these skills in different formats will help your child master the basics of mathematical thinking.

What Will You Find in *Space Math*?

With *Space Math* children will have fun looking for patterns in the night sky, learning to predict the phases of the moon, and figuring out their weights on other planets. They'll also learn some amazing facts about the planets and use problem-solving skills to help a group of weightless astronauts deal with sleeping, eating, and playing in space.

On a sunny day, go outside with your child and see how the sun's position in the sky changes the length and direction of your shadows. On a moonlit night, take a close look at the shape of the moon and see if you can predict what the next phase will be. Or imagine yourself on another planet: How hot or cold is it there and how much would you weigh?

We hope you and your child will enjoy your journey through *Space Math* and will both say:

I LOVE MATH!

The Editors
Time-Life for Children

Look at page 42 to see how I crack a code in space and save the day.

Table of Contents

THE SEARCH FOR THE MYSTERY PLANET

"Cousin Ferd and Cousin Erkna sure know how to throw a good party," said Moop.

"Sending us out into space on a treasure hunt was a great idea," said Gork. "We have almost everything on the list, at least all the things from our solar system: a dregack from Relegar 7, a snorf from the planet Quork, and a rock from the second moon of Endorf."

"Now all we need," said Moop, "is a petunia and a poodle. We must search for a mystery planet that has land, water, oxygen and carbon dioxide, enough sunlight, and a temperature around 70 degrees. You know, 70 degrees is a temperature that lots of living things like."

Moop looked out the window. "I see a planet now," she said. "I'll ask the computer to send out its electronic probe and give us a printout with information about this planet."

"According to the computer, this planet is called Pluto," said Gork. "Pluto has land," he continued, "but the water is all frozen, the air has no oxygen or carbon dioxide, there's not enough sunlight, and the temperature is not around 70 degrees. The sun is so far away its rays are very weak when they reach Pluto. So this is the wrong planet. We need a planet with a 'yes' for every number."

● ●

MYSTERY PLANET

1. Land
2. Water
3. Oxygen and carbon dioxide
4. Enough sunlight
5. 70° temperature

PLUTO

1. Land: Yes
2. Water: Yes, but frozen
3. Oxygen and carbon dioxide: No
4. Enough sunlight: No
5. 70° temperature: No

Explain to your child that a day on a planet is how long it takes the planet to rotate once on its axis, and that a year is how long it takes the planet to go once around the Sun.

Pluto is seen rising above its moon Charon. The Sun is so far away that it looks no bigger than a bright star in the dark sky.

MORE FACTS ABOUT PLUTO. Pluto, the farthest planet from the Sun, is a ball of ice and rock that is smaller than the Earth's moon. With temperatures never rising above −350°F, Pluto is the coldest planet in the Solar System.

As Moop and Gork searched for the mystery planet, they came upon a huge blue planet. It was much bigger than Pluto. Gork sent out the electronic probe to see if this planet could possibly have a petunia and a poodle living on it. He asked the probe about the five important things that living things need. The message that came back looked like this.

● ●

MYSTERY PLANET	**NEPTUNE**
1. Land	1. No
2. Water	2. Yes, but frozen
3. Oxygen and carbon dioxide	3. No
4. Enough sunlight	4. No
5. 70° temperature	5. No

● ●

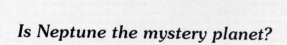

Neptune is the windiest planet in the Solar System. On this stormy planet, winds can reach 1500 miles per hour!

Is Neptune the mystery planet?

MORE FACTS ABOUT NEPTUNE. A year on Neptune is equal to 165 Earth years. Each of Neptune's 4 seasons lasts 41 Earth years. If you went to school on Neptune, you'd have a very long summer break!

SPACE QUIZ. If the dregack eats 5 kurrs and the
snorf eats 3 kurrs, how many kurrs did they eat
altogether?

Moop and Gork left Neptune and traveled on in their search for the mystery planet.

"What does a petunia look like, anyway?" asked Gork.

"You've got me there," said Moop. "And what is a poodle? Is it something to eat?"

As Moop and Gork looked out their window they saw another planet.

"Wow!" said Moop. "It's tilted way over on its side. I hope this is the planet we're looking for."

"Hope again," said Gork as he looked at the printout.

• •

MYSTERY PLANET	URANUS
1. Land	1. No
2. Water	2. Yes, but frozen
3. Oxygen and carbon dioxide	3. No
4. Enough sunlight	4. No
5. 70° temperature	5. No

• •

Is Uranus the mystery planet?

MORE FACTS ABOUT URANUS. It takes Uranus 84 Earth years to go once around the Sun. Because it goes around on its side, half of the planet is bathed in light for 42 Earth years while the other half is plunged in darkness for the same length of time!

10

Uranus is the only planet that goes around the Sun on its side.

SPACE QUIZ. If there are 3 zoqs of water and the snorf drinks 1 zoq, how many zoqs of water are left?

Still on the lookout for the mystery planet, Moop and Gork continued their journey.

"Maybe this is the place we're looking for," said Moop as they flew past a big, beautiful planet.

"Wowee zowee! Look at the size of it, and look at all the rings," Gork exclaimed.

"Yeah. The rings are beautiful, and they're kind of glittery," said Moop. "Let's go around this one a couple of times. I don't want to miss anything."

"I counted 18 moons here, and some of them are inside the rings," said Gork. "Let's get the computer printout and see if this is the mystery planet."

• •

MYSTERY PLANET	SATURN
1. Land	1. No
2. Water	2. No
3. Oxygen and carbon dioxide	3. No
4. Enough sunlight	4. No
5. 70° temperature	5. No

• •

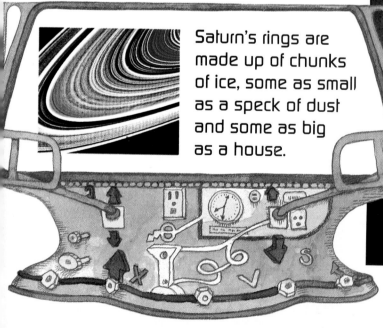

Saturn's rings are made up of chunks of ice, some as small as a speck of dust and some as big as a house.

Is Saturn the mystery planet?

12

MORE FACTS ABOUT SATURN. Although Saturn is about 9 times bigger than Earth, it is lighter than water. It would float if you could find a pool of water big enough to hold it!

Sometimes pictures of Saturn's rings are artificially colored so you can see the individual rings.

SPACE QUIZ. If Moop has 6 trisks and Gork has 4 trisks and they give away 2, how many trisks are left?

"Moop, come here quick! Look at the size of this planet!" shouted Gork.

"Kookamonga! It's even bigger than the last one. Do you think we can land on it?" asked Moop.

"Let's send down the probe and find out," said Gork.

They were amazed by what the probe found. "Why, this planet is just a big ball of gas," said Gork. "It doesn't have any solid ground for us to land on."

• •

MYSTERY PLANET	JUPITER
1. Land	1. No
2. Water	2. Yes, but frozen
3. Oxygen and carbon dioxide	3. No
4. Enough sunlight	4. No
5. 70° temperature	5. No

• •

"Look at that big red spot. I wonder what that is," said Moop. "I'm sure the computer will have something to say about it. Let's have a look."

Jupiter's Great Red Spot is an enormous storm that has been raging for more than 300 years.

Is Jupiter the mystery planet?

14

MORE FACTS ABOUT JUPITER. Three Earths could fit inside Jupiter's Great Red Spot. A day on Jupiter is the shortest of any planet, about 10 Earth hours long, but its year is more than 11 Earth years long.

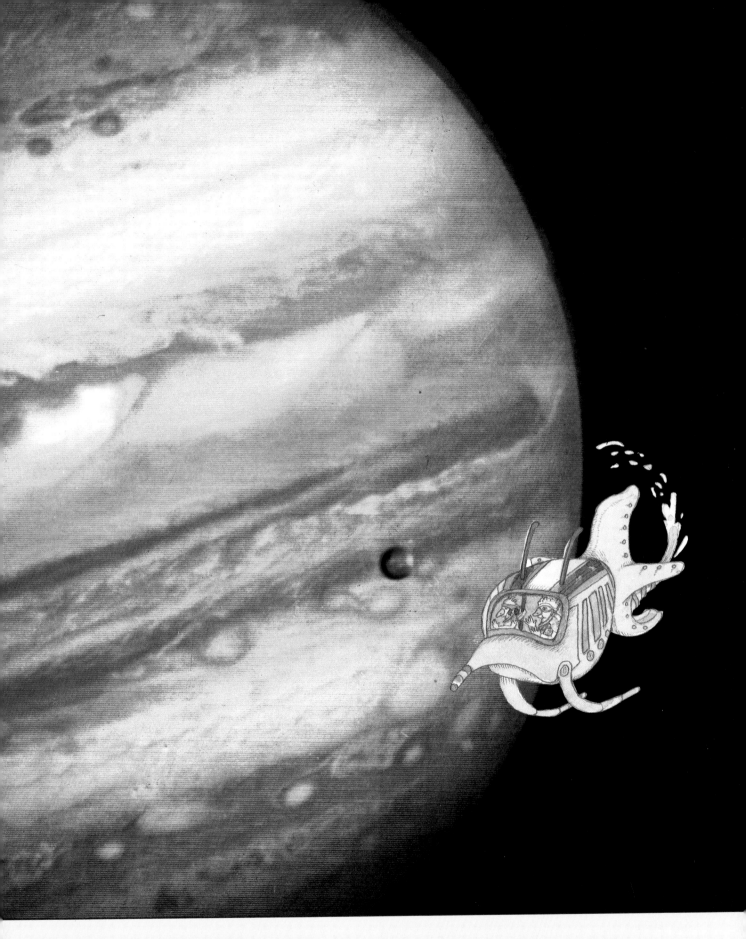

SPACE QUIZ. If the probe has 5 lights and 2 of
them break, how many lights are still working?

15

"Wow! A red planet," exclaimed Gork. "It looks solid to me. I wonder if it has land."

"We'd better check the printout and also compare it to our list," said Moop.

● ●

MYSTERY PLANET	MARS
1. Land	1. Yes
2. Water	2. Yes, but frozen
3. Oxygen and carbon dioxide	3. No oxygen
4. Enough sunlight	4. Yes
5. 70° temperature	5. Yes

● ●

"I think we can land and go out for a walk," Moop said.

"Will we need our spacesuits?" asked Gork.

"We'd better wear them," answered Moop. "The computer says there are a lot of powerful dust storms on the planet, so we should protect ourselves."

Mars is called the Red Planet because of the red rust-like dust that covers its surface.

Is Mars the mystery planet?

16

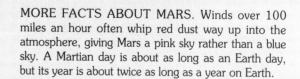

MORE FACTS ABOUT MARS. Winds over 100 miles an hour often whip red dust way up into the atmosphere, giving Mars a pink sky rather than a blue sky. A Martian day is about as long as an Earth day, but its year is about twice as long as a year on Earth.

SPACE QUIZ. If a Marzak is 9 feet tall and a Marmak is 10 feet tall, how much taller is the Marmak?

Gork was very tired after his walk on Mars. As they continued their flight, he took a nap.

"Wake up! Wake up!" cried Moop. "Look, Gork, look at the printout! This could be the mystery planet!"

● ●

MYSTERY PLANET	EARTH
1. Land	1. Yes
2. Water	2. Yes
3. Oxygen and carbon dioxide	3. Yes
4. Enough sunlight	4. Yes
5. 70° temperature	5. Yes

● ●

"Let's land and see if there are any petunias or poodles here. I'm hungry."

"Let's not be in such a hurry," said Gork as he rubbed the sleep out of his eyes. "I want to see if there are any more planets in this solar system that have 5 'yes' answers. Let's check and see. Then we can come back to this one."

"OK," said Moop, who was always willing to explore new places. So off they went.

The Earth is called the "big blue marble." About three-quarters of the planet is covered by water, giving it its blue color.

18

Why did Moop think that Earth might be the mystery planet?

MORE FACTS ABOUT EARTH. Earth is precisely positioned in our solar system so it has the ideal conditions for life. If it were any closer to the Sun we would fry up. If it were any farther away, the planet would freeze into a ball of ice.

SPACE QUIZ. If Moop has 12 grackies and she loses 9 of them, how many grackies are left?

19

The two space travelers had decided to take a walk on the next planet, even though the computer said it was really hot. They knew their suits would protect them. So down they went like the brave explorers they were.

They landed their spaceship and walked about on the yellow planet for a short while. But it was hard to walk. The air was so heavy that it felt like they were walking under water.

"Poodles, schnoodles," said Moop. "I'm out of here."

"I'm right behind you," Gork said.

● ●

MYSTERY PLANET	**VENUS**
1. Land	1. Yes
2. Water	2. No
3. Oxygen and carbon dioxide	3. No oxygen
4. Enough sunlight	4. No, heavy cloud cover
5. 70° temperature	5. No

● ●

Venus is the hottest planet in the Solar System. Thick clouds keep the Sun's heat from leaving Venus.

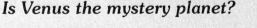

Is Venus the mystery planet?

MORE FACTS ABOUT VENUS. Temperatures on Venus can reach as high as 900° F, which is more than twice as hot as an oven gets when you bake cookies. A day on Venus is longer than a year there, so you would have a birthday at least once a day!

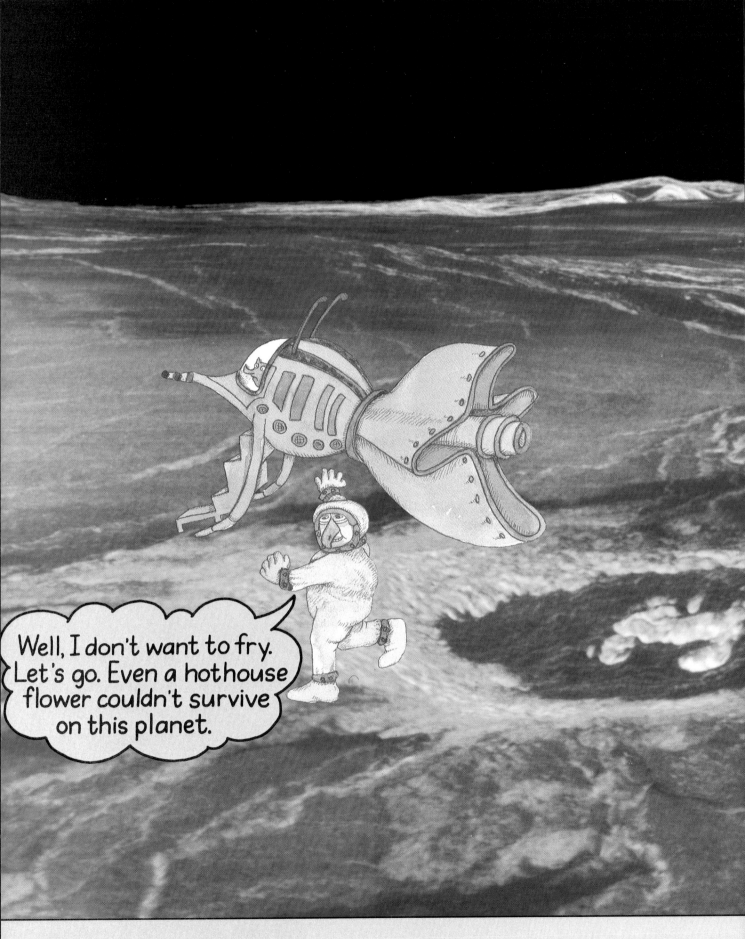

SPACE QUIZ. If Gork has 2 bowls and puts 3 gegs
in each bowl, how many gegs does Gork have in all?

They flew on to the last planet, Mercury.

"Let's check the data on the computer printout and see if this last one could be the mystery planet," said Moop.

"OK," said Gork as he punched the keys that sent down the probe.

● ●

MYSTERY PLANET	**MERCURY**
1. Land	1. Yes
2. Water	2. Yes, but frozen
3. Oxygen and carbon dioxide	3. No carbon dioxide
4. Enough sunlight	4. Yes
5. 70° temperature	5. No

● ●

"Now that we've seen all nine planets in this solar system, I think I know where to find the petunia and the poodle," said Gork. "But to be sure, let's check all the data first."

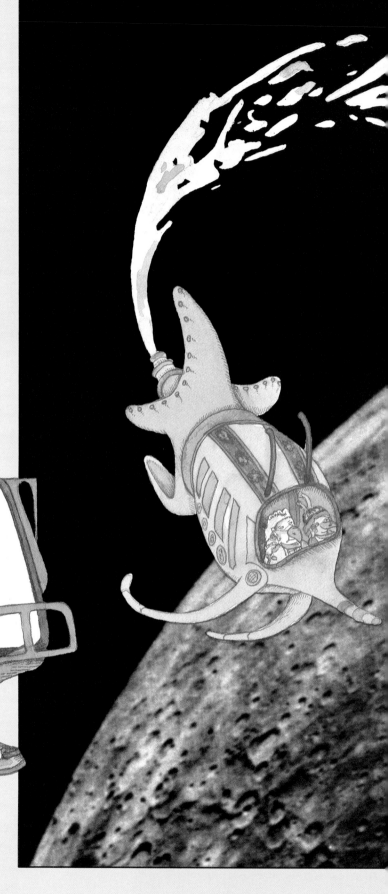

Mercury is one of the hottest and coldest planets. Temperatures go way up to 800° F during the day and way down to −300° F at night.

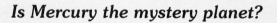

Is Mercury the mystery planet?

MORE FACTS ABOUT MERCURY. Mercury spins very slowly on its axis, making for very long days and nights and great temperature extremes. The time between sunrise and sunset is equal to 3 Earth months. Only 3 days go by every 2 years on Mercury!

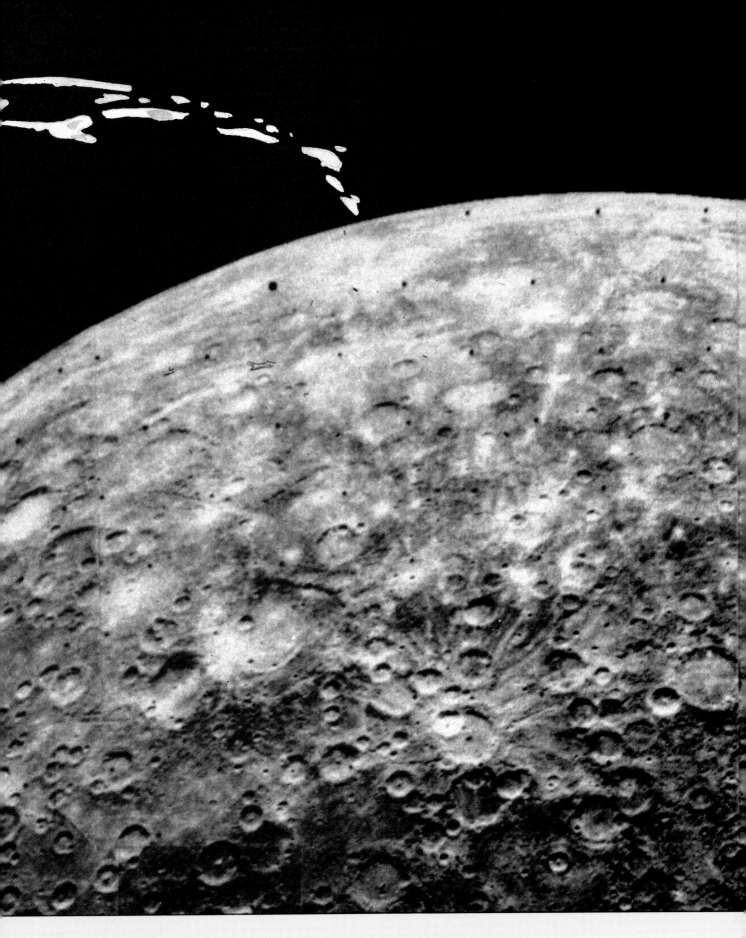

SPACE QUIZ. If Gork eats 7 merknuts and Moop eats
2 more merknuts than Gork, how many merknuts did
Moop eat?

PLANET	LAND	WATER	OXYGEN AND CARBON DIOXIDE	ENOUGH SUNLIGHT	70° TEMPERATURE
Pluto	Yes	Yes, but frozen	No	No	No
Neptune	No	Yes, but frozen	No	No	No
Uranus	No	Yes, but frozen	No	No	No
Saturn	No	No	No	No	No
Jupiter	No	Yes, but frozen	No	No	No
Mars	Yes	Yes, but frozen	No oxygen	Yes	Yes
Earth	Yes	Yes	Yes	Yes	Yes
Venus	Yes	No	No oxygen	No, heavy cloud cover	No
Mercury	Yes	Yes, but frozen	No carbon dioxide	Yes	No

How many planets have water?
How many planets have both oxygen and carbon dioxide?
Which planet could have a petunia and a poodle on it?

Dear Ferd and Erkna,
Having a wonderful time.
Wish you were here.
Will keep in touch.

       Love,
       Gork and Moop

P. S. If you have 10 klonks
and a Gredak eats 3
of them, how many
klonks do you have left?

Ferd and Erkna
Planet Lom
Mol Galaxy

Our Solar System

The planets in our solar system revolve around the Sun. This is a chart showing the planets close to the Sun, the planets very far from the Sun, and the ones in between. It also shows the Asteroid Belt between Mars and Jupiter. Do you know the name of the planet we live on?

...to	Neptune	Uranus	Saturn	Jupiter
...er of ...s: 1	Number of moons: 13	Number of moons: 14	Number of moons: 18	Number of moons: 16

MATH FOCUS: SPATIAL SENSE AND ORDINAL NUMBERS. By exploring the positions of the planets in relation to the Sun, children focus on the relationships of objects in space. Explain to your child that Neptune, Uranus, and Jupiter all have very thin

rings that cannot be seen in most photographs. The rings can be shown here because this is an artist's painting. Pluto is not always the farthest planet from the Sun; sometimes its path crosses in front of Neptune so Neptune becomes the farthest planet.

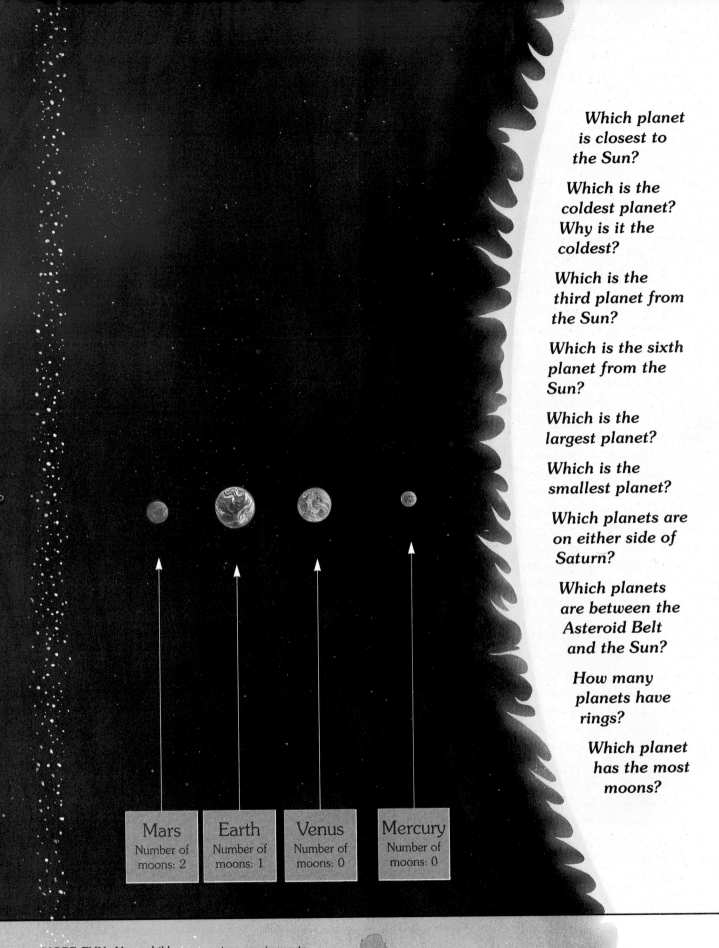

Which planet is closest to the Sun?

Which is the coldest planet? Why is it the coldest?

Which is the third planet from the Sun?

Which is the sixth planet from the Sun?

Which is the largest planet?

Which is the smallest planet?

Which planets are on either side of Saturn?

Which planets are between the Asteroid Belt and the Sun?

How many planets have rings?

Which planet has the most moons?

Mars
Number of moons: 2

Earth
Number of moons: 1

Venus
Number of moons: 0

Mercury
Number of moons: 0

MORE FUN. Your child can create a sentence to help remember the order of the planets: for example, *Most Ventriloquists Eat Marshmallow Jellybeans Slowly Until None Pop.*

LIFTOFF!

Everything has been checked. All systems are A-OK. In exactly one minute the rocket boosters will ignite and the space shuttle will lift off the ground. Everyone watching is unbelievably excited. It's T minus 60! The letter T stands for "launching time." So "T – 60" means there are 60 seconds until liftoff. Instead of beginning with 1 and counting to 60 the people watching count backwards from 60 to 1 and then yell, "Liftoff!" They watch a clock that marks the seconds backwards.

Try it! Pretend you are in a spaceship or a rocket ready for launching. It's T – 60. Remember, you're going to count 60 seconds backwards. Ready? Go: 60, 59, 58, 57 and so on to 1

and

LIFTOFF!

MATH FOCUS: MULTIPLICATION READINESS AND COUNTING AND GROUPING. By counting backwards from 60 to 1, children practice counting skills that are essential for ordering and comparing numbers.

Tell your child that boosters are extra rockets attached to a rocket ship to give it extra power at liftoff. When they ignite, the booster fuel catches fire and the boosters push the rocket up.

You just counted backwards from 60 to 1 by ones. Try counting back from 60 by tens. Then count back by fives. Try counting back by twos. You can use this chart to help you.

1	2	3	4	5	6	7	8	9	10
11	12	13	14	15	16	17	18	19	20
21	22	23	24	25	26	27	28	29	30
31	32	33	34	35	36	37	38	39	40
41	42	43	44	45	46	47	48	49	50
51	52	53	54	55	56	57	58	59	60

MORE FUN. Your child can count backwards from 100 by ones, twos, fives, and tens.

MOON Math

Have you ever seen a full moon? Beautiful, isn't it? But the moon doesn't always look full. Sometimes you see the moon in a different shape. All of the moon's shapes are called phases of the moon. The phases are grouped in quarters. Each quarter is about 7 days long. There are about 7 days from the first quarter to a full moon. There are about 7 days from a full moon to the last quarter. There are about 7 days from the last quarter until there is no moon in the sky. Then there are about 7 days until the next first quarter. What will the moon look like tomorrow night? What will it look like in 7 days?

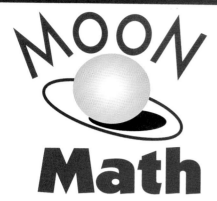

1 **2**
First Quarter

8 **9**
Full Moon

15 **16**
Last Quarter

22 **23**
New Moon

MATH FOCUS: ELAPSED TIME, THE CALENDAR, AND PATTERNS. By learning about the phases of the moon, children strengthen their understanding about the passing of time.

Tell your child that there are 7 days in a week and about 4 weeks in a month.

3   4   5   6   7

10   11   12   13   14

17   18   19   20   21

24   25   26   27   28

MORE FUN. Ask your child how long it is from one
full moon to the next. You and your child can track
the phases of the moon by watching the night sky or
finding the phases on a calendar or in a newspaper,
or you can make your own moon calendar.

# My **S**hadow

Have you ever seen your shadow walking along with you on a sunny day? Your shadow looks like you, doesn't it? Except your shadow changes size and it isn't always in the same place. Have you ever wondered why? Your shadow is made when light from the Sun is blocked by your body. As the Sun moves across the sky it changes the position of your shadow and makes it longer or shorter. Here's a simple experiment you can do to see for yourself. You will need a spot outside on some pavement that will stay sunny all day long.

MATH FOCUS: SPATIAL AWARENESS AND LENGTH. By seeing how the changing position of the Sun in the sky affects the position and length of shadows throughout a day, children get hands-on measuring experience.

32

Go outside early in the morning when the Sun is still low in the sky. Stand on the pavement with your shadow in front of you. Have someone draw around your shadow with a piece of chalk. Where is the Sun in the sky? Does your shadow lean to your right or to your left? Now use a tape measure to measure your shadow. How long is it?

Go outside again at noon, when the Sun is high in the sky. Stand in exactly the same place. Have someone draw around your shadow again. Measure your shadow. How is your shadow different from the one in the morning?

Do the same thing late in the afternoon, when the Sun is again very low in the sky. Where is the Sun now? Where is your shadow? Look at the three outlines of your shadow. When was your shadow the longest? When was it the shortest?

CAUTION! Never look at the Sun. It is so hot and bright that it could burn your eyes and blind you.

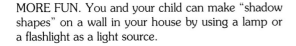 MORE FUN. You and your child can make "shadow shapes" on a wall in your house by using a lamp or a flashlight as a light source.

The Daily Dill

Showing Up

RELISH SALE: PICKLES PANIC

Pickles Crash on Asteroid

The Jarship landed with several loud bangs and a thump that shook it from stem to stern and sent Piccalilli and Gherkin rolling to the side of the cabin.

"Where are we? What happened?" asked Gherkin as he picked himself up. "The floor's slanting and I can hardly stand up straight."

"We've crash-landed on a small asteroid and just in time, too!" answered Piccalilli. "The fuel tank is completely empty."

"I think we've got more trouble than that," said Gherkin. "We should go out and see what damage has been done. I'm sure I heard some tires blow out on the right side as we hit the asteroid."

"You're right," said Piccalilli. "I don't relish going outside on a strange asteroid, but we must find out what happened."

The pickles put on their spacesuits and opened the Jarship's lid. Then they let down the steps and bravely went out to inspect the ship.

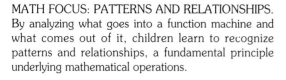

MATH FOCUS: PATTERNS AND RELATIONSHIPS. By analyzing what goes into a function machine and what comes out of it, children learn to recognize patterns and relationships, a fundamental principle underlying mathematical operations.

34

Tell your child that finding each order is like finding the reason why the objects that go in and come out "go together."

"What can we do?" sighed Gherkin.

Piccalilli sat and thought for a minute. "I've solved the problem!" she cried. "Well, almost. It's Uncle Picklepuss's letter. I was just starting to read it when we crashed."

"Explain, please. You don't compute," said Gherkin, still worried. "How can a letter fix a tire?"

"Uncle Picklepuss's letter says that he put a Function Machine in the Jarship. He thought it would come in handy. Boy, was he right or what?" crowed Piccalilli.

"I still don't understand," complained Gherkin.

"Come on! You will," said Piccalilli.

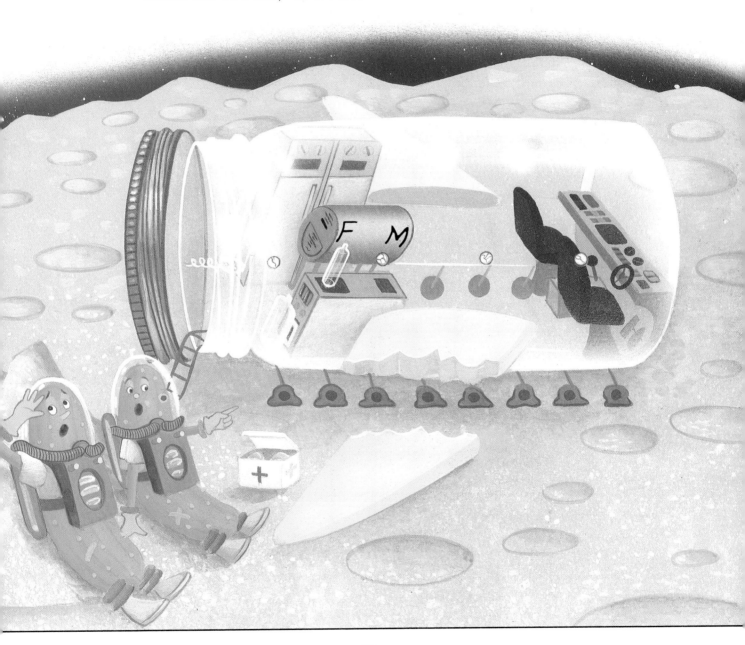

MORE FUN. Encourage your child to make up his or her own orders for the function machine, telling what he or she would put into the machine and then telling what would come out.

The pickles set up the Function Machine, and Piccalilli showed Gherkin how it works.

"When you put an order in this slot," explained Piccalilli, "the machine will do whatever the order tells it to do."

"First," she said, "let's solve our fuel problem. I'll write the order and put it in the Function Machine here."

"Where do I stand?" asked Gherkin.

"At the other side," said Piccalilli. "You stand and the FM will deliver."

Piccalilli puts an empty fuel bottle into the FM.

What happened?

Piccalilli puts three empty fuel bottles into the FM.

Tell what happened.

What order did Piccalilli give to the machine?

Piccalilli puts another order into the left side of the FM. Gherkin waits on the right side.

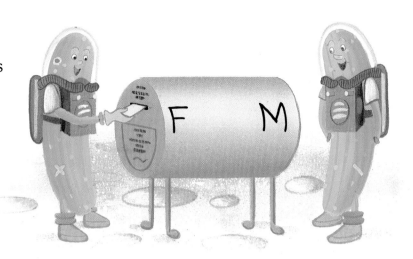

Piccalilli puts a tube of Jarship-wing glue into the FM.

What happened?

Tell what Piccalilli is doing with the air tanks.

Tell what happened.

What order did Piccalilli give to the machine?

Piccalilli put another order into the machine.

Tell what Piccalilli is doing.

Tell what happened.

Tell what Piccalilli is doing.

Tell what happened.

What order did the machine follow?

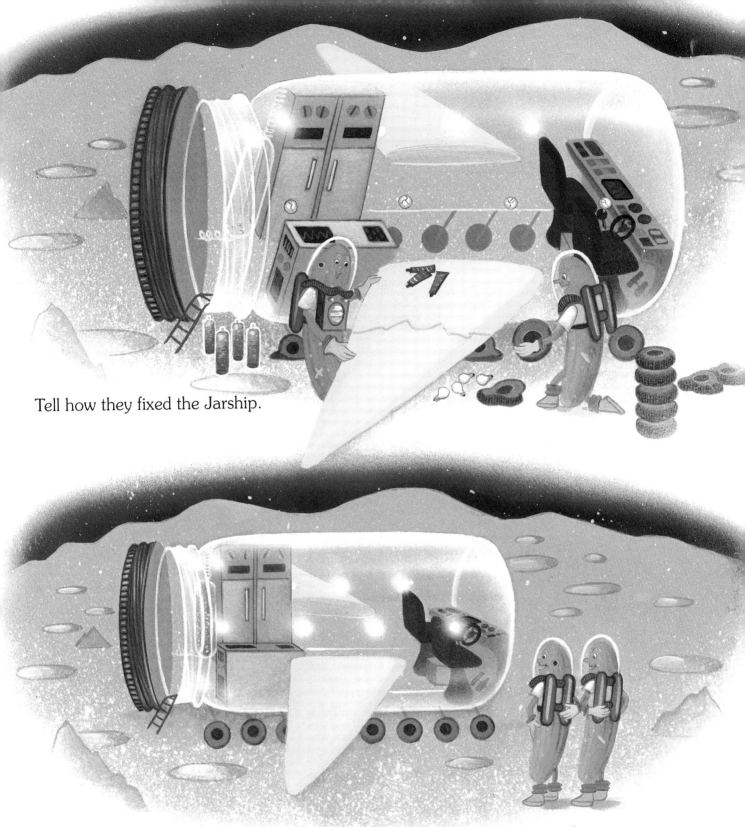

Tell how they fixed the Jarship.

"Everything's fixed," said Piccalilli. "We can go home now."

"This was fun. Can the FM do anything besides fix Jarships?" asked Gherkin.

"A function machine can follow any order you give it," said Piccalilli. "It can even use numbers."

"Let's try," said Gherkin. "I love doing this!"

Piccalilli put another order into the machine.

What is Piccalilli putting in?

What is Gherkin taking out?

What is Piccalilli putting in?

What is Gherkin taking out?

If 0 is put in, what number will come out?
Now count backwards from that number and
watch Piccalilli and Gherkin lift off for home.

The Case of the Mystery Message

Professor Guesser was strapped into her seat on the spacecraft. She could hear the countdown from Mission Control in her ear. "5, 4, 3, 2, 1. We have ignition. LIFTOFF!"

She closed her eyes, held her breath, and clutched the nearest thing she could get her paws on. The noise was deafening as the enormous booster rockets fired.

In a cloud of fire and smoke, the spacecraft lifted off the launch pad. Up, up, up it went. Soon the booster rockets and the external fuel tank were jettisoned. They were cast off from the ship.

Professor Guesser opened her eyes and saw part of the far-off Earth through the spacecraft window.

MATH FOCUS: PATTERNS AND RELATIONSHIPS. By listening to a story about a coded message, children analyze the patterns and relationships of symbols and letters in a code.

Help your child work out the code on page 47. Guide him or her to see the pattern of tens and ones, with a * representing 1 and a # representing 10.

At last the spacecraft was in orbit around Earth. Professor Guesser watched as the crew moved weightlessly around the cabin doing the work they were sent into space to do. The professor had been invited on this flight as a civilian observer. She was a perfect choice because of her natural curiosity. And she planned to observe as much as she could.

The crew's job was to put a new weather satellite into space. Professor Guesser watched them on the control panel screen. She felt useless. She wanted to help, but she was only an observer. So she listened to the radio as she observed the crew.

Then Professor Guesser began to hear a series of blips and beeps. The noise was faint at first, then it got louder.

"Do you hear that?" she asked.

But the other astronauts were too busy to answer her.

MORE FUN. Your child can make up a mystery message using the code on page 47 and challenge family members to solve it.

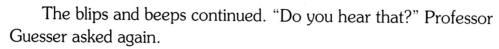

The blips and beeps continued. "Do you hear that?" Professor Guesser asked again.

"It could be a signal from the weather satellite," said one of the astronauts as she wrote down some data in her log.

"But why would we hear it?" asked the professor.

"The radio could be picking up the signal," said the astronaut. "I don't think it's anything important."

But the blips and beeps continued. Professor Guesser was worried. "It sounds to me like the signal is repeating every minute or so," said Professor Guesser to another astronaut.

"It could be a special kind of star, a pulsar, that the radio is monitoring," he said. "When I'm finished taking these photographs, I'll look into it."

The blips and beeps were getting stronger. "I think someone is trying to tell us something," said Professor Guesser to Commander Nova. "It sounds like a message in code."

"Major Quota is our code expert," replied the commander. "But he's too busy fixing the control-panel lights to decode this message right now."

Professor Guesser gave herself a job. She would decode the message herself. The professor took out her ever-present notebook.

Professor Guesser listened carefully to the blips and beeps and wrote what she heard in her notebook. She wrote until the message began to repeat.

"My feline instinct tells me that if someone is trying to tell us something they will use a code that is easy for us to break." She examined the blips and beeps. "There are never more than 9 blips, and never more than 2 beeps. Maybe each beep stands for 10 blips. Then the code could have as many as 29 different patterns. An alphabet code would have to have 26 patterns and it would be the easiest way to communicate. So the blips and beeps probably stand for letters of the alphabet." Professor Guesser quickly wrote down the alphabet and assigned a pattern of blips and beeps to each letter.

* = blip   # = beep

A *	N #****
B **	O #*****
C ***	P #******
D ****	Q #*******
E *****	R #********
F ******	S #*********
G *******	T ##
H ********	U ##*
I *********	V ##**
J #	W ##***
K #*	X ##****
L #**	Y ##*****
M #***	Z ##******

Then Professor Guesser began to decode the message:

Can you decode the message?

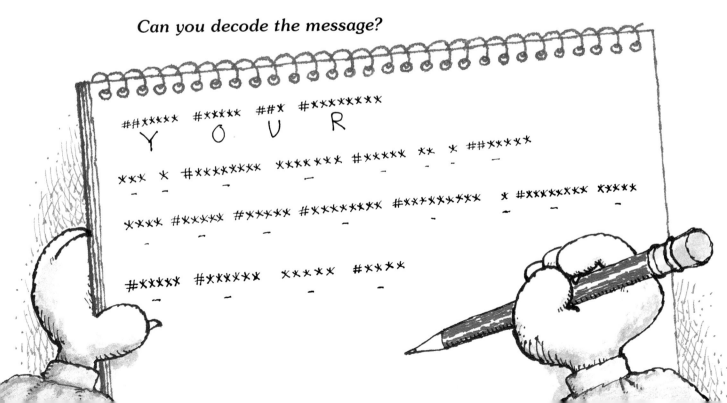

##*****   #*****   ##*   #*********
  Y   O   U   R

***   *   #*********   *******   #*****   **   *   ##*****

****   #*****   #*****   #*********   #*********   *   #********   *****

#*****   #******   *****   #****

YOUR CARGO BAY DOORS ARE OPEN

With their mission successfully completed, the astronauts were preparing the spacecraft for its return to Earth when Professor Guesser started yelling excitedly.

"Quick! Check the cargo bay doors! They must have stayed open after you launched the satellite!" she shouted.

"The doors are open? Why didn't the warning light go on?" asked the alarmed commander.

"The light's broken," said Major Quota. "We wouldn't have known about the doors if the professor hadn't decoded the message!"

"Thank you, Professor Guesser! You've saved the day!" said Commander Nova. "It would have been extremely dangerous if we had reentered the Earth's atmosphere with the cargo bay doors open."

Just then a strange-looking spaceship zoomed by.

"That must be the UBO that sent the message!" exclaimed P.G.

"Don't you mean UFO, unidentified flying object?" asked the major.

"No," replied Professor Guesser. "It was a UBO, an unidentified beeping object!"

More Mystery Messages

Here are some more words to decode.

Here's a code key to help you decode some mystery words that rhyme with "moon."

YOU SEE:	1	2	3	4	5	6	7	8	9	10	11	12	13	14	15	16	17	18	19	20	21	22	23	24	25	26
THE REAL LETTER IS:	A	B	C	D	E	F	G	H	I	J	K	L	M	N	O	P	Q	R	S	T	U	V	W	X	Y	Z

Mystery Words

14 15 15 14   10 21 14 5

19 16 15 15 14   19 15 15 14

20 21 14 5   2 1 12 12 15 15 14

This code is a little trickier. Try to decode the mystery words, which rhyme with "sun."

YOU SEE:	A	B	C	D	E	F	G	H	I	J	K	L	M	N	O	P	Q	R	S	T	U	V	W	X	Y	Z
THE REAL LETTER IS:	Z	A	B	C	D	E	F	G	H	I	J	K	L	M	N	O	P	Q	R	S	T	U	V	W	X	Y

Mystery Words

G V O   X P O   C V O

E P O F   S V O   U P O

C F H V O   P O F   O P O F

MORE FUN. Your child can use one of the codes to make up words that rhyme with *star*.

Weigh Out!

When you jump up off the ground, do you ever wonder what brings you back down to Earth? An invisible force called gravity pulls you down.

The moon has gravity, too, but its gravity is not as strong as the Earth's. On the moon you'd be able to jump much higher before you were pulled back down.

How much higher? About 6 times higher. Let's say you can jump off the Earth 1 foot. How high could you jump off the moon?

MATH FOCUS: WEIGHT, LARGER NUMBERS, AND CHARTS. Children read a chart and use larger numbers to find out how much they would weigh on different planets.

Explain to your child that a range of "51 to 60" includes 51, 52, 53, 54, 55, 56, 57, 58, 59, and 60. Help your child use the chart on pages 52 and 53.

Gravity also affects how much you weigh. When you weigh yourself, gravity pulls your body down on the scale. The stronger the gravity, the more you weigh. The weaker the gravity, the less you weigh. Would you weigh more or less on the moon than you do on Earth?

How much does this boy weigh on Earth?

How much would he weigh on the moon?

Did you know that your weight would be different on other planets than it is on Earth?
That's because gravity is stronger on some planets than on others.

Use this chart to find out about how much you would weigh on another planet.
First, weigh yourself so you know how much you weigh on Earth. Then find the box in the white Earth column that shows your weight "range." A "range" is two numbers that stand for themselves and all the numbers in between. To find your weight range on other planets, look at the different-colored boxes in the same row.

For example, the boy on these pages weighs 60 pounds on Earth. His weight falls within the 51-60 range in the white Earth column. He would weigh between 19 and 23 pounds on Mars and between 130 and 152 pounds on Jupiter.

About how much would you weigh on Mars and Jupiter?

On which planet would you weigh the least?

On which of the planets would you weigh the most?

Would you weigh the same on any two planets?

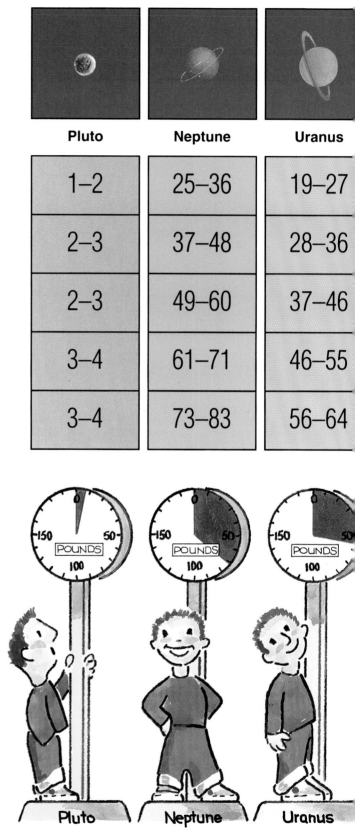

Pluto	Neptune	Uranus
1–2	25–36	19–27
2–3	37–48	28–36
2–3	49–60	37–46
3–4	61–71	46–55
3–4	73–83	56–64

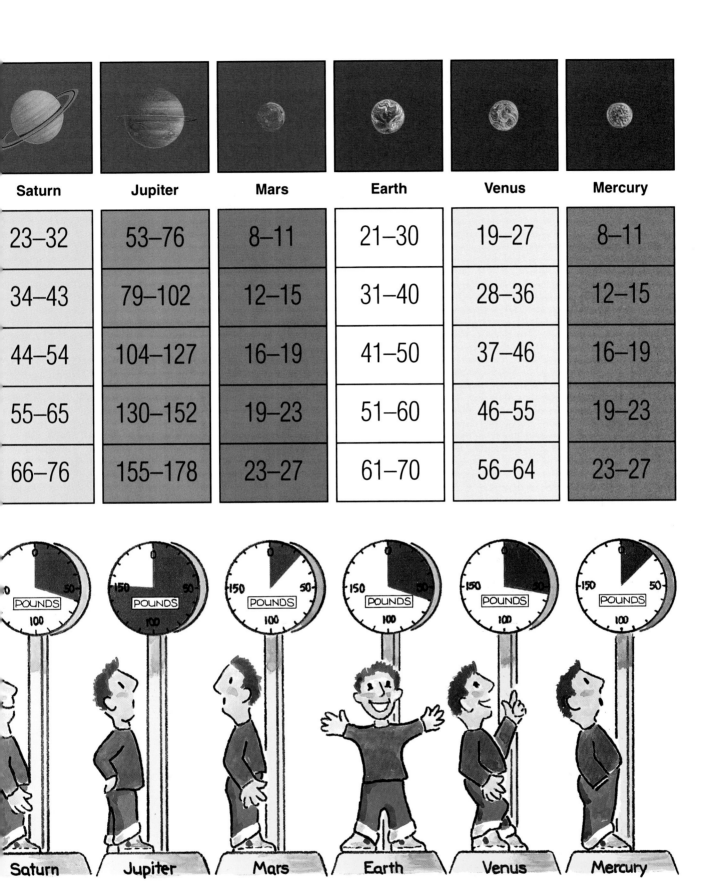

Saturn	Jupiter	Mars	Earth	Venus	Mercury
23–32	53–76	8–11	21–30	19–27	8–11
34–43	79–102	12–15	31–40	28–36	12–15
44–54	104–127	16–19	41–50	37–46	16–19
55–65	130–152	19–23	51–60	46–55	19–23
66–76	155–178	23–27	61–70	56–64	23–27

Get It Together!

What would living in space be like? Everything would be weightless most of the time, including you! You could walk on walls or sit on the ceiling if you wanted to. If you dropped a glass it wouldn't fall to the floor and break. It would just float in the air.

Spaceship life could be fun, but it could also be difficult. Just look at the problems the people in this spaceship are having. How would you help them to . . .

play checkers in space?
eat peas?
keep a sandwich together?
lie flat to sleep?
wash their faces?
drink juice?

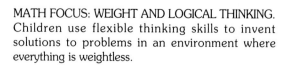

54

MORE FUN. Here are some ways NASA solves these weightless problems: Velcro is used to attach things to surfaces; food is made sticky so it doesn't float around; straws are used to drink beverages; water comes out of hoses with trigger nozzles; and toothpaste is digestible so it doesn't have to be spit out.

What's a Googol?

A TEN is your toes
And a TEN is your fingers.
A HUNDRED's a choir,
Ten rows with ten singers.
A THOUSAND is daffodils,
Yellow and pretty.
A MILLION is people
Who live in a city.
A BILLION is snowflakes
That cover the ground.
A TRILLION is stars,
Up above, all around.
BUT . . .
A GOOGOL's a googol.
A googol is great!
It has one hundred zeros,
Not seven or eight.
A googol's enormous:
It's more than the stars,
It's more than the snowflakes,
Or the distance to Mars.
A googol's a number
That you'll never count.
You'll never discover
A googol amount.

I didn't know how powerful we zeros are! Without us a googol wouldn't amount to much.

10,000,000,000,000,000,000,000,000,000,000

56

MATH FOCUS: COUNTING AND GROUPING OF LARGER NUMBERS. By exploring very large numbers in a humorous way, children gain a greater understanding of our numeration system.

Tell your child how many zeros each of the following numbers has: ten — 1, hundred — 2, thousand — 3, million — 6, billion — 9, trillion — 12. Explain that infinity is an unlimited amount so it cannot be counted.

000,000,000,000,000,000,000,000,000,000,000,000,000,000,000,000,000,000,000,000,000,000,000,000

So why have a googol?
A googol is fun.
Can you imagine
A googol of gum,
A googol of polka dots,
A googol of noodles,
A googol of pizza,
A googol of poodles?
A googol's a number
As huge as can be.
And though it is big,
It's not infinity.

But what do you call a googol of cows-a moogol?

MORE FUN. Your child might enjoy the following
riddles. *What do you call a googol of ghosts?*
(a boogol) *What do you call a googol of feet?*
(a shoogol) *What do you call a googol of animals?*
(a zoogol)

57

Star Patterns

Long ago people gave names to patterns made by groups of stars in the night sky. In this picture an artist has connected the stars in a few patterns to show what people imagined long ago.

Find all the patterns without a closed part. Next, find all the patterns with a closed part. Tell how many corners each closed part has. How many lines does each closed part have?

Find all the patterns with a long tail. Find the ones without a long tail.

Find all the patterns with a kite shape. Then find the ones without a kite shape.

Point to two patterns. How are they alike? How are they different?

Which star group has the greatest number of stars? Which has the fewest? Do any two groups have the same number of stars?

Star patterns, clockwise from top left: **URSA MAJOR,** ALSO CALLED "GREAT BEAR." THE BIG DIPPER IS PART OF URSA MAJOR. **URSA MINOR,** ALSO CALLED "LITTLE BEAR," AND "THE LITTLE DIPPER." **CASSIOPEIA,** WHO ACCORDING TO MYTH WAS AN ETHIOPIAN QUEEN. **CYGNUS** THE SWAN. **PEGASUS** THE WINGED HORSE. **ORION** THE HUNTER, WITH HIS 3-STAR BELT. **GEMINI** THE TWINS.

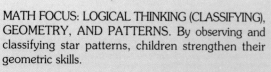

MATH FOCUS: LOGICAL THINKING (CLASSIFYING), GEOMETRY, AND PATTERNS. By observing and classifying star patterns, children strengthen their geometric skills.

58

Tell your child that star patterns like these are called constellations.

Create Your own Star Patterns

Cover some of these stars with thin white paper and mark the stars you want to use in your pattern. What shape do you see? Draw lines to show the shape. Give your star pattern a name.

Does your star pattern have a closed part? How many big, bright stars does it have? Make up a story for your star pattern.

MATH FOCUS: GEOMETRY AND PATTERNS. By creating their own star patterns, children get hands-on experience in making geometric shapes and observing patterns.

60

Have available crayons and thin white paper. Encourage your child to use his or her imagination when creating his or her star pattern and the story about it.

MORE FUN. Help your child create a 3-D star pattern by making holes in one end of an empty oatmeal container. Then he or she can shine a flashlight in the container to see the star pattern on a wall or on the ceiling.

61

MATH FOCUS: LOGICAL THINKING AND ADDITION. By using a calculator to play a game, children practice adding while using reasoning skills to figure out a winning strategy.

Tell your child that both players use the same calculator. Play this game with your child, remembering to press = after each turn.

MORE FUN. You and your child can play a different version of this game. Start with 50 on the calculator. Take turns subtracting a number from 1 to 9. The first player to reach 0 wins.

TIME-LIFE for CHILDREN®

Publisher: Robert H. Smith
Associate Publisher and Managing Editor: Neil Kagan
Assistant Managing Editor: Patricia Daniels
Editorial Directors: Jean Burke Crawford, Allan Fallow,
   Karin Kinney, Sara Mark, Elizabeth Ward
Director of Marketing: Margaret Mooney
Product Managers: Cassandra Ford,
   Shelley L. Schimkus
Director of Finance: Lisa Peterson
Financial Analyst: Patricia Vanderslice
Administrative Assistant: Barbara A. Jones
Production Manager: Prudence G. Harris
Production: Celia Beattie
Supervisor of Quality Control: James King

Produced by Kirchoff/Wohlberg, Inc.
866 United Nations Plaza
New York, New York 10017

Series Director: Mary Jane Martin
Creative Director: Morris A. Kirchoff
Mathematics Director: Jo Dennis
Designer: Jessica A. Kirchoff
Assistant Designers: Brian Collins, Mike Hortens,
   Daniel Moreton, Judith Schwartz
Contributing Writers: Anne M. Miranda, Dr. Helene
   Joy Silverman
Managing Editor: Nancy Pernick
Editors: Susan M. Darwin, Beth Grout, David McCoy

Cover Illustration: Rosekrans Hoffman
Cover Photograph: NASA/JPL

Illustration Credits: Diane Blasius, front end papers(silhouette);
Liz Callen, pp. 28–29, 32–33, 54–55; Rosekrans Hoffman,
pp. 6–25; Mike Hortens, pp. 50–53; Tom Leonard, pp. 26–27,
34–41; Don Madden, pp. 42–49; Arvis Stewart, pp. 58–59;
Troy Viss, pp. 60, 62–63.

First printing. Printed in U.S.A.
Published simultaneously in Canada.

Time Life Inc. is a wholly owned subsidiary of THE TIME INC.
BOOK COMPANY

TIME-LIFE is a trademark of Time Warner Inc. U.S.A.

For subscription information, call 1-800-621-7026.

CONSULTANTS

Mary Jane Martin spent 17 years working in elementary
school classrooms as a teacher and reading consultant; for
seven of those years she was a first-grade teacher. The
second half of her career has been devoted to publishing.
During this time she has helped create and produce a wide
variety of innovative elementary programs, including two
mathematics textbook series.

Jo Dennis has worked as a teacher and math consultant in
England, Australia, and the United States for more than 20
years. Most recently, she has helped develop and write
several mathematics textbooks for kindergarten, first grade,
and second grade.

Judy Heard is an elementary school teacher in the public
school system of Fairfax County, Virginia. She was a first-
grade teacher for almost 14 years, and currently teaches
math in grades 1 through 6. In 1990, she was awarded the
Virginia Elementary Math Teacher Award by the Virginia
Council of Teachers of Mathematics. In 1991, the National
Science Foundation presented her with the Presidential
Award for Excellence in Teaching Elementary Mathematics,
an award given each year to one teacher from every state.

Thomas A. Lesser is an author and lecturer on astronomy
and the space sciences and formerly was the Senior Lecturer
at the American Museum–Hayden Planetarium.

Photography Credits: All photos are from NASA/JPL
except the following: page 7, David Hardy, Science Photo
Library, Photo Researchers; 11(bkgd.), Harvard College
Observatory; 16, U.S. Geological Survey; 25, H. Veiller,
Explorer, Photo Researchers; 30, Hale Observatory, Hansen
Planetarium; 54–55(bkgd.), Royal Observatory, Edinburgh;
56–57, Lick Observatory, University of California.

Marsball

The Number of Players: 2–4

The Object of the Game: To be the first to get a score of 20 or more.

The Playing Pieces: A die; a different "Marsball" for each player, such as a coin or a button; and paper and pencil for scoring.

The Play: Players are having a kicking competition on Mars. Each player places his or her Marsball on "Start." The first player rolls the die, doubles the number shown, and places his or her Marsball on that space on the playing field. (Since the gravity on Mars is only about half as strong as the gravity on Earth, the ball would go about twice as far on Mars.) After each player has had a turn, players move their Marsballs back to "Start" and play another round.

Scoring: If the Marsball lands in the yellow section the player gets 1 point. If it lands in the red section the player gets 2 points, and if it lands in the blue section the player gets 3 points. Use a pencil and paper to keep track of your score after each turn.

The Winner: The winner is the first player to get 20 points or more.

Math Concepts: Multiplication readiness. Addition and subtraction.